Ben Lost a Tooth

By Leslie Kimmelman

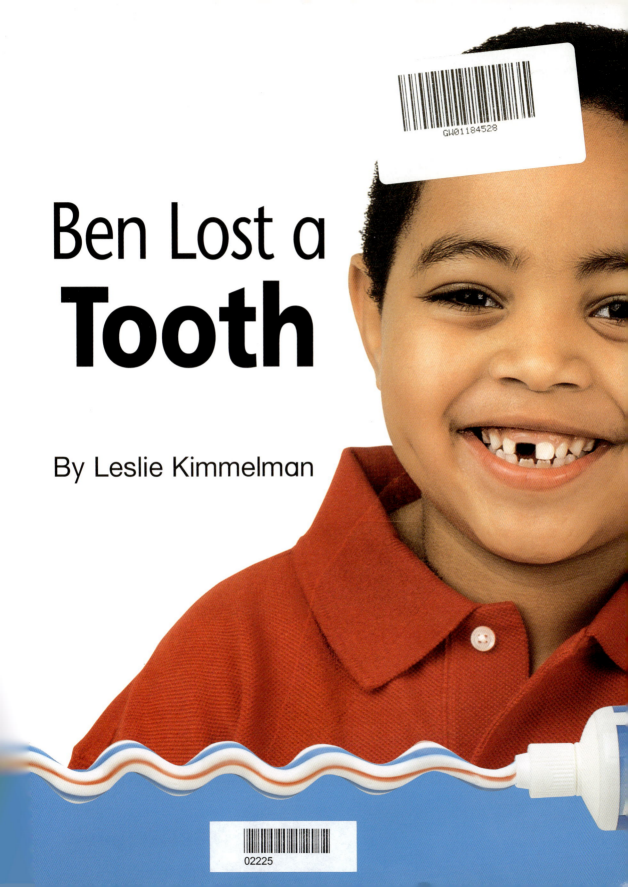

Once Ben had no teeth.

Now Ben has lots of teeth.

Ben had a loose tooth.

baby tooth

Ben's tooth came out!

new tooth

A new tooth grew in its place.

Now another tooth is loose.

How Ben Takes Care of His Teeth

 He brushes his teeth.

 He flosses his teeth.

 He visits the dentist.

 He eats healthy foods.